Jessica and the Moonflower Fairies

Jessica and the Moonflower Fairies

Carla Daniel

To order additional copies of this book, contact:
Xlibris Corporation
1-888-795-4274
www.Xlibris.com
Orders@Xlibris.com
45656

Contents

DEDICATION

This book is dedicated to Rachael my beautiful goddaughter that has come back into my life, and to my husband who continues to encourage my writing and my wonderful children Amber(for her editing, Patricia(for her encouragement), Casey(for the beautiful illustrations) and Amanda(who drew the pretty little fairy in chapter 2). A special thanks to all of my great friends who have encouraged and made this book happen, Joanna, Gidget, Cyndi, BW and Shalena and too many to mention. I wish a very special thank you to my mother Levina Vogel for her great illustrations and to Terrence Ragsdale for the amazing graphics on the cover of the book.

Chapter 1

The Moonflowers

Jessica was an average eight-year-old girl—not a special girl at first sight. She had brown hair, green eyes, and a big pretty smile. Jessica was very smart. She loved to read books. She would read about everything and anything. That is how our story begins.

Jessica and her family were in Georgia, staying at their summerhouse. It was a nice area, and Jessica had met a couple of friends the year before. She was hoping they would get there soon, so that she would have someone to play with. Jessica was an only child, and she got bored easily. The neighborhood consisted of about twelve houses lined up in a neat row. There was a wildflower field just behind Jessica's backyard. Katie, a girl she had met last year, lived next door; and Joey, Katie's cousin, lived across the street. They each lived in different states during the school year, but their families came to Georgia for the summer.

Jessica was lying in her bed that lazy hot summer evening when the doorbell rang. It was Katie and Joey, her best friends; they had come to let Jessica know that they had arrived and to see if Jessica wanted to play soccer. Katie was ten and Joey was nine years old. Jessica felt it was too hot for soccer and asked her friends if they would like to take a walk instead. The children agreed, and so they set off for a nice evening walk. As they walked, Katie noticed a pretty flower and wondered out loud what it was. "That is a magnolia," stated Jessica. Katie knew when she asked her thought out loud that Jessica would tell her what it was. Katie sometimes liked to see just how smart Jessica was. And Jessica was always happy to show her.

As they walked around the corner, there was a large field. Many wildflowers grew in the field. Joey saw white flowers that were growing on a vine, nearly twelve feet tall. And the strong fragrance was unlike anything he had smelled before. Joey could not help himself; he turned to Jessica and asked what it was. "It looks like a morning glory, but the flowers are so white and smell so good. All the rest of the morning glories have closed up for the day." Jessica smiled; she knew it was something special when Joey would ask her a question. He hated it when she knew everything and would nearly never ask her anything that would show she was smart.

"Those are moonflowers," stated Jessica. "They are always white and smell so strong as to attract small bats, butterflies, and moths. They only bloom at night. Tomorrow night, if we come back earlier around 5 p.m., maybe we will be able to watch them when they open. I have read that it is a real sight to see."

Jessica, Katie, and Joey continued with their walk. They decided to go to the community playground. The children ran and played. They climbed on the monkey bars and swung on the swings until everyone was hot and exhausted. Finally, they decided they had better get home before their parents came out looking for them. When Jessica got to her house, she was so hot and sweaty that without even being told to, she went straight to the bathroom and started a nice cool bath. After her bath, Jessica decided to read some more books on moonflowers and morning glories. *You can never know enough*, she thought.

Before Jessica realized it, it was 11 p.m. She turned off the light and fell sound asleep. Jessica had the most wonderful dream of running through fields of wildflowers complete with the morning glories and moonflowers.

When Jessica woke up it was nearly 10 a.m. Her mother was in her room gathering up dirty laundry to wash. Jessica's mother was complaining to Jessica about staying up too late reading again and that she was sleeping the day away. Jessica got up, got her robe, and went downstairs for breakfast. She poured herself a bowl of cereal and some orange juice. She was so excited about going to see the moonflowers open that evening that she could hardly wait. *Today was going to be the longest day of my life*, thought Jessica.

Katie called about that time and said, "My mom is taking me and Joey with her to the mall. Would you like to come?"

"Oh yes! I would love to!" shouted Jessica. *At least now I will have something to do*, she thought. Jessica ran back upstairs to get dressed for the mall. Jessica had put on a green sleeveless blouse and black shorts and stepped into black sandals. She pulled her hair up into a mint green ponytail, and was ready to go. Katie's mom pulled up into the drive, and Jessica's mom yelled to Jessica that they were there to get her. Jessica was already coming down the stairs.

When Jessica got into the car, Joey started laughing. Jessica looked up surprised, and then looked at Katie. Katie was staring at Jessica too. They were wearing exactly the same clothes. Katie began to laugh and exclaimed, "We look like twins." Katie's mother asked the girls if they had planned what they were going to wear. The girls giggled and said, "No they had not."

When they got to the mall, the girls wanted to go look in Claire's Jewelry Store, and Joey wanted to go to the sporting goods store. Katie's mother insisted that the kids could go look around the mall without her and meet back at 3 p.m. at the snack bar, but they would have to stay together. Katie and Jessica decided they would go with Joey first to the sporting goods store and then he agreed he would go with them to the jewelry store after.

Jessica and Katie purchased some really pretty crystal necklaces; even Joey thought they looked cool. The crystals were a pretty light pink shade and hung from a white string. If you held the crystals up to the light, they would reflect many colors around the room like a rainbow.

The girls looked at the clock and realized it was nearly 3 p.m. so they headed with Joey to the snack bar. Katie's mom was already waiting at the snack bar when they got there. The girls showed her the necklaces. "Wow," said Katie's mom. "Those are very pretty." The girls showed her how they would reflect the rainbow. Joey was a little disappointed since he did not buy anything at the store. But there just wasn't anything he really wanted, or that he had enough money to buy.

When the kids got home, they dropped off Jessica. Jessica reminded the others to be at her house at four thirty sharp that evening, and they would go to the field. Jessica went inside and changed into some play clothes. Her mother was yelling upstairs that she could not go back out until her room was clean and her bed was made. Sometimes it seemed her mother had the world's worse timing. But Jessica knew that if she planned to be ready to leave in an hour, she had better get busy. She made her bed and picked up all the books and restacked them on the bookcase. She put away the basket of clean clothes her mother had left in her room for her. Before she knew it, it was already 4:30

p.m. Katie and Joey were knocking on the front door.
Jessica told her mom the room was done and asked
if she could go out with Katie and Joey. They barely
listened for her to say yes, and they were on their way
out the door.

When the children got to the field, they laid out
the blanket they had brought with them in front
of the moonflowers. They sat down to wait. After
about ten minutes and nothing had happened so far,
Jessica decided to tell the others about her dream. "It
was so wonderful. It was evening just like this; and I
was running through all the wildflowers, and I saw
butterflies everywhere. So many more than what we see
here now. There must have been hundreds." Then all
of a sudden, Katie shouted, "Look!" And the children
saw the moonflowers were all starting to open. They
all began to open at exactly the same time. And just
when they were nearly open they made a *pop* sound.

It was the coolest thing you could ever see. And they smelled so pretty.

"Do you know what would be really great?" asked Katie.

"No what?" asked Joey and Jessica at the same time.

"Let's come back tomorrow night and bring a camera. I can borrow my dad's digital, and we can get them developed at the photo store."

Every one agreed it was a good idea. So they headed home for supper and planned to meet in the morning to prepare for the photo shoot that next evening.

The next morning Jessica was up and dressed at 8 a.m., waiting for her friends.

"Wow," said her mom, "you are up and dressed early today."

Jessica told her mother all about the moonflowers and their plan to take pictures as the flowers opened up that evening. Her mother stated she thought it was a good idea and even suggested that maybe they could take the pictures as the flowers open and then put them together, and it would be like a film of the flowers opening up. Jessica really liked her mom's idea and decided to tell the others about it. As Jessica finished her breakfast, Katie and Joey showed up. Katie had her dad's camera as she had promised. They practiced all morning taking pictures of each other. They ate lunch together and decided to go swimming for a while in the afternoon to help the time pass by. Finally, it was time to head for the field.

When the children got to the field, they spread their blanket out again in front of the moonflowers just as they had the day before. Joey noticed some morning glories were open still not far from where the moonflowers were growing. He saw a beautiful monarch butterfly on the morning glory; it was pollinating the flower. I wonder if the butterfly will pollinate the moonflower too or not. Jessica had read that the butterfly will pollinate, both but not so much after dark since that is when the moths comes out to eat, and as they eat, they pollinate the flowers. The moths are attracted by the sweet smell of the moonflowers.

Suddenly the moonflowers all began to open. "Hurry," shouted Jessica and Joey. "They are opening, get the camera." Katie was ready; she began to take pictures right away. She snapped the pictures one right after another as fast as she could, until *pop*, the flowers were all opened. The camera had a view on it that the kids could see the pictures and she how they turned out. It was very small, but it gave you an idea of how they would look. The children all agreed that the pictures would be fine. Suddenly, a lunar moth hovered above the moonflower.

"What is that?" asked Joey.

"I think that is a lunar moth," stated Jessica. "But I thought they did not come out until after dark. That one is a sphinx moth. They are also called hummingbird moths even though they are not birds; it is because of the way they hover like a hummingbird over the flower. The lunar moth is flying around the flower. Take a picture of it, Katie. It may be a rare picture for this time of day. And I don't see any other of them out here at all."

Katie took the picture, and they got ready to head home for supper.

The next morning, the phone rang at 9 a.m. It was Katie; she was so excited that Jessica could not understand what Katie was even saying. "Just come over right away, and I'll show you!" shouted Katie. Jessica agreed and got up and got dressed. She went downstairs and got a pop tart. She asked her mom if she could go to Katie's. Jessica's mom said yes, and so Jessica headed out the door. Since Katie lived next door, it did not take her long to get there. Katie was still very excited when Jessica walked in the door. "Come on," said Katie. "I have to show you something."

When they got upstairs to Katie's room, Katie pulled out the pictures. Her dad had taken her to the photo store early that morning to get them developed.

"That moth is a fairy, not a moth!" shouted Katie.

"Okay, you have lost your marbles," suggested Jessica. "Take a look at the picture, and you will see what I mean. Wait, you need to use the magnifying glass."

Jessica looked at the pictures, and she could not believe her eyes. How could this be? There is no such thing as fairies. Yet looking at the picture, Jessica now understood why Katie had been so excited. They called Joey and told him to come over right away. Joey knew there had to be a logical explanation. Fairies were in fairy tales not in their field. He told the girls they would have to catch one if it showed up again, and then they would know for sure. Joey had taken lots of pictures and knew that sometimes things looked different on camera than they really were. They planned to meet that evening in the field.

At four thirty, they spread their blanket out on the ground. It was just past 5 p.m. when the moonflowers did their evening show for them. They could never see that show too often. It was the most splendid sight. And just as suddenly, the moth showed up. They looked at her, but she looked like a plain old moth. Joey had brought a jar with a lid. He had cut holes in the lid so the moth/fairy could breathe. And then Joey snatched it so fast the moth did not even know what was happening. The children looked very closely, and the moth looked at them—it was a fairy.

Chapter 2

The Fairy

The fairy appeared to be afraid. She looked up at the children, and they noticed she had tears in her eyes. Jessica right away felt sorry for her. "We won't hurt you," she promised. "We took a picture of you. What we thought we saw when we took the picture was a moth and then the picture of you showed a fairy. So we had to capture you and see what you really were.

We did not even know that fairies existed. We'll release you right away."

"Wait!" shouted Joey. "Don't let her go. She may give us wishes or something."

However, Jessica knew that letting the fairy go was the right thing to do. So she opened the lid to the jar and let her go. The fairy flew out of the jar right away and disappeared.

Then just as suddenly, the fairy came back again. The children were all very surprised, and they just stood there staring at the fairy.

"Don't just stand there," she said. "Come on, let's go. We have adventures to find."

The shocked children did not move. Did the fairy really come back? And is she really inviting them on adventures?

Finally, Katie snapped out of it and said, "Where do you want us to go?"

The fairy explained to them that her name was Ambrosia. That is a name in ancient mythology that the gods gave their pets. Pet was her mother's nickname for her. Jessica liked the fairy's name even though it was a pet name.

"Well, what are your names?" asked the fairy.

"Oh, I'm sorry," Jessica said. "We did not mean to be so rude. We really were just so surprised about you coming back. My name is Jessica. This is Katie, and he is Joey."

"Okay," said the fairy, "we are ready to go."

The fairy was quite beautiful; she was still only the size of a moth but had very delicate features. Her wings were a pretty light green color and her lips were a light shade of pink. Now that Jessica looked closer, she saw the fairy had blue eyes and black hair. Somehow this just surprised Jessica even more. She leaned over and whispered to Katie to look at how beautiful the fairy's eyes were. Katie agreed and also pointed out that the fairy was wearing a dress that was the exact same color as her wings so that you could hardly tell where her body stopped and her clothes began. She was truly an amazing creature.

Jessica, Katie, Joey, and the fairy all headed for the field.

"Where are we going?" asked Katie.

"I want to show you my home," said the fairy.

The fairy's home turned out to be the middle of the field. The fairy called out in a strange small voice. Suddenly, the field became alive with butterflies and moths everywhere. As the moths and butterflies came close to the children, they could tell they were all fairies. The fairies buzzed all around the children. They seemed to be just as excited as the children.

"Fly with us," the fairies called.

"We can't fly," the children exclaimed.

"Can the bats carry them?" the butterfly fairies asked.

"Bats!" yelled the children all at once. "We are not going near bats."

"Why?" asked Ambrosia.

"They bite," stated Jessica, "and they are really mean."

"No," stated Ambrosia, "not these bats. They are called nectar bats, and they are gentle. They only eat fruit, and they help us to pollinate the moonflowers. But you are far too heavy for the bats. They carry us around if one of us is sick or injured."

It was getting late and the children knew they would be in trouble if they did not get home, so they said good-bye to the fairies and promised to return the next evening. Ambrosia told the children they could not tell anyone about them. If they did, the adults and other children would come to the field and catch them all and keep them as prisoners. The children said they understood and promised they would not tell anyone. And they left to go home.

It was a lot harder than they had thought not telling their families about the fairies. But they had promised, and they intended to keep that promise. When Jessica's mom asked her what she had been doing all day, Jessica stated they had gone to the field and played in the wildflowers. This was not a lie, and Jessica did not feel bad telling her mom. Katie did not have it so easy. Her parents wanted to know a little more. How could the children spend so long just playing in a field of wildflowers? Katie explained to her parents how they watched the moonflowers open, and about the sphinx and the lunar moths and the monarch butterflies. Her parents were even more impressed when Katie told them about the nectar bats that only eat fruit and help the moths and butterflies pollinate the moonflowers. Katie's father was so surprised; he did not know that Katie had such an interest in nature. Katie was glad when they were satisfied with that and did not ask any further questions. Joey's dad was so glad that Joey had behaved all day and stayed out of his way so he could watch the football games that he never even questioned Joey. The children were all exhausted and fell asleep quickly that evening.

The next morning, Katie came to Jessica's house very early. She was so excited she could not wait to talk to Jessica about the evening before.

"What do you think the fairy moth meant by 'we have adventures to go on'?" Katie asked.

"I don't know, but I think just finding the fairies was the biggest adventure I can imagine," Jessica stated.

"What do you think will happen if we go this evening?" asked Katie.

"What do you mean *if*? We are going to go, aren't we?" asked Jessica.

"Of course," said Katie. "I guess I'm just a little worried about what they meant about adventures. You do think they are friendly, don't you?"

"Yes, I think they are," Jessica said. "We have to go back. We can learn so much from them about their lives. We have to go."

"Okay," said Katie, "we will go, but let's be careful."

The girls heard a loud knock on the door. It startled them both since they were so deep in thought about the fairies. Jessica heard her mom say, "The girls are upstairs. You can go up." They knew immediately it had to be Joey. Joey came into the room and started talking about the fairies.

"I have had to keep it inside of me for so long. I could hardly wait to see you two so I could start talking about them. It is so hard to keep a secret that is so exciting. Although I am sure that if we were to tell anybody they would think we were crazy and would not believe us anyway."

Chapter 3

The Surprise Dew

Jessica, Katie, and Joey continued to talk about the fairy moth and about all the fairy friends in the wildflower field. Joey was thinking out loud about how the fairies looked like moths and butterflies from a distance. About how you had to be so close to really tell the difference, or how the field seemed so quiet with very few of them until the moth called out in that strange little voice and suddenly the field came alive with moths and butterflies. Jessica and Katie had been thinking the same thing. They all had to laugh about it. This was the best secret they ever had.

"I wonder why anyone would ever want to capture them," Jessica said. "I just don't understand. They really seemed afraid of being captured."

"Well," said Katie, "it does make sense. I mean, after all, wouldn't everyone love to have their own fairy. They are fairies, not just moths and butterflies." And they all had to agree.

Katie and Joey had to go home for breakfast, and they had chores to do or they would not be allowed out this evening. Jessica said good-bye and went downstairs for her breakfast. After breakfast, Jessica helped her mom clean house, and they worked together to do the laundry. They went grocery shopping and then went home to put it all away. Katie had left a message on Jessica's answering machine. Katie wanted to know if Jessica wanted to go to a movie to help pass the day. The movie started at one and it was now twelve fifteen. Jessica asked her mother if it would be okay, and then called Katie and told her yes. Katie and her mom showed up about fifteen minutes later and picked Jessica up.

The movie was good. It was a comedy and really did help to pass the time. Jessica's mother said they were eating supper early because her dad had to go out of town and they wanted to eat before he left. They were going to eat at 5 p.m. That will mess up everything.

Jessica complained, "We like to be at the field at four thirty." *Okay*, thought Jessica, *let's see how can I make this work*. Jessica decided to call Katie and Joey, and invite them to supper. That way, they could stay at the field later without having to hurry home for supper. Jessica asked her mother if they could eat over. When her mom said yes, she hurriedly called the others and invited them along with an explanation of how it would work. At four fifteen, the children showed up for supper. They could hardly stay calm as they ate. They were so anxious to go back to the field. After supper, Jessica gave her father a hug and said good-bye, and they were on their way to the field.

When the children arrived at the wildflower field, they did not see any moths or butterflies at all. They became very worried. What if something had happened to them? Or maybe they were afraid the children could not keep such an important secret, and so they decided to leave before the children could tell anyone.

Suddenly there was a loud swooshing, and the field became alive with the buzzing of moths and butterflies. It was such a beautiful sight. The children were so relieved.

"What happened? Where were you all a few minutes ago?" asked Jessica.

Ambrosia, the lunar moth they had first met, explained, "We had to be sure it was you before we showed ourselves. We were just being careful. Now it is time to tell you another secret. Tomorrow morning you must meet us here at 6 a.m., no later. We have an exciting adventure to take you on."

"What is it?" the children all asked at once.

"We can't tell you yet. It would ruin the surprise, but I can tell you it will be a lot of fun. Now first we can go through the field, I want you to meet more of my family and friends," Ambrosia told the children.

The children were very anxious to know what was in store for them in the morning. But they did as the moth told them and went about the field, meeting her family and friends. Everyone was so nice to them. They would introduce the children to more and more moths and butterflies.

"One day," said Ambrosia, "I will tell you more about the lunar moths, but that will have to wait for another day. It is getting late now, and you will need to get a good-night's sleep for your big day tomorrow. We will say good-bye for now. Don't forget, you must be here no later than 6 a.m. for the surprise."

"Bye," said the moths and butterflies. The children thought they could hear some giggles from some of the young butterflies and moths. The children yelled good night and headed home. They all went straight to bed and could hardly wait for morning.

Jessica's alarm went off at 5 a.m. She had already told her mother that she and Katie and Joey were going to the field at 6 a.m. for an experiment they were doing. She was surprised her mom did not ask for more details. Katie and Joey's parents also said they could go. At fifteen minutes till six, everyone was ready, and so they headed to the field.

When they got there, they immediately saw moths hovering above a moonflower, pollinating it as they had so many times before. As soon as the lunar moth saw the children, she came right over. She was very excited to see them.

"Are you ready?" she asked.

"Yes, I think so," the children said. What are we going to do?"

"Come on, and I will show you," she told them.

She took the children immediately to the moonflowers.

"It is a beautiful morning, and the moon is full so this will be perfect."

The children continued to stare nervously at the moth fairy.

"Drink the dew in the moonflower," she told the children.

"Why?" they asked.

"You will be able to fly with the fairies," explained the moth fairy. "This can only be done in the early morning when the dew is fresh in the moonflowers, before they die. Moonflowers only bloom once, and then they drop off the vine," the fairy explained. "It is such a magical time. Drink the dew and fly with me."

The children were nervous. Jessica knew the moonflowers were poisonous, especially the seeds, but drinking the dew from the flower should be safe. "Okay," she decided and took the first sip. The other children watched to see what would happen.

Suddenly she felt so light and could feel herself lifting off the ground. She spread her arms and found that she could fly anywhere she wanted too.

"You can't go too far," said the moth fairy. "You have to stay near the moonflowers for it to work, but that means anywhere in this field."

Katie and Joey took their sips of dew from the moonflowers. Soon all three of them were flying all around the field.

The moth fairies and butterfly fairies all flew around, above, and below them. It was magical. They were having so much fun they did not realize the sun had risen so high in the sky.

Slowly the children began to lower to the ground.

"The time is up for flying," explained the lunar moth fairy. "The night is over, but the moon will be in the full setting for two more nights. If you can come again early like you did today, you will be able to fly with us again."

The kids said they definitely would come back early like they had this morning. They decided not to go home right away. They just sat back and watched the butterflies as they went from morning glory to morning glory.

The moonflowers were all gone for the day. And now it was time for the morning glories to show their beauty. From where the children watched, the butterfly fairies looked like beautiful monarch butterflies. It was such a wonderful sight—and what a wonderful secret they had. Soon the children got hungry, and had to say their good-byes, and headed home for lunch.

Chapter 4

The Nectar Bats

It was nearly 4 p.m. when Katie came over to Jessica's house.

"Where is Joey?" Jessica asked.

"I have not seen him since we left the field earlier today," Katie said.

The girls decided to call Joey and see what he was doing.

Joey had been building a birdhouse. Well, that is what he told his dad. It was actually a fairy hiding house for a surprise gift. Joey wanted to give the fairies a place to rest where maybe nobody would find them. Or at least it would be a cool place to relax during the heat of the day. Jessica and Katie both thought it would be a great idea.

"Don't tell the fairies about the houses. They won't be ready for a while, and I want it to be a surprise when we give the houses to them." The girls agreed not to say anything.

"Are you ready to go to the field?" they asked. "We want to watch the moonflowers open." Joey was ready and agreed to be over in five minutes.

When the children arrived at the field, they did not see any moths or fairies at all. The children knew that the fairies would hide until they were sure of who had come to the field. The children spread out the blanket in front of a particularly large vine of moonflowers. Katie looked around the field.

"Something is wrong," she said.

"What do you mean?" Jessica asked.

"I don't know I just feel that something is desperately wrong."

Jessica and Joey noticed at that moment that still no moths or butterflies were around.

"You don't think they are mad at us, do you?" asked Jessica.

"No, I think it is something else. Let's go take a look around."

The children forgot all about the moonflower as they grew concerned for the fairies. They began to walk around the field.

Katie yelled, "Come quickly."

It was Ambrosia; she was hiding in a hole of a tree.

"What is wrong?" they asked.

"After you kids had left, we did a head count, and from the night before we were missing thirty fairies again. Some were moths and some were butterflies. Someone is coming and taking us away, and we can't figure out who or what it could be. They are very sneaky; we never see them. The butterflies seem to be taken the quickest that is why they are not out. I was hiding here where I had tried to get some sleep. We think the capturing is being done at night. Oh, I wish you could stay all night and help us catch the fairy-nappers in the act."

The children said they would ask their parents if maybe they could spend the night.

The children all raced home to ask their parents if they could go camping in the wildflower field. At first, the parents were very hesitant, but since the field was practically right in Jessica's backyard, the parents all decided it would be okay.

Joey and Katie's dads went into their sheds and came out with two tents. They set up a small tent for Joey to sleep in and a slightly larger tent for the girls. "You cannot start a campfire tonight since there will not be any adult supervision." The children agreed and gathered snacks and sodas to take for the stakeout. It was going to be a long night. The children wondered what was going to happen tonight.

When they arrived at the field, the tents were already up and waiting for the children. They were excited and nervous at the same time. The children's parents stayed for a while to make sure they would be all right.

Finally, after what seemed like an eternity, the parents left; and Ambrosia came out to see the kids. The children decided to put their sleeping bags outside the tents, and then they could pretend to be asleep and lay there and watch to see who or what showed up.

At last, it was time. They lay down in the sleeping bags and watched. The sphinx moths would hover from moonflower to moonflower. There were still some butterflies out, but most had gone to sleep for the night. Suddenly, there was a whoosh; something much larger than the butterflies and moths was flying around. At first the children became frightened. But they continue to lie real still and watch.

Finally, they realized it was a nectar bat. It landed on a moonflower near the kids and began to drink from it. At last, it went to a butterfly. The butterfly, after a moment or two, climbed on the bat's back, and the bat flew away. After a while another bat, or possibly the same one, came back and got a moth to climb on its back, and away it flew again. When it left, the children whispered, "That has to be it. But Ambrosia said the bats were their friends, why would the nectar bats be taking them away?"

"I don't know, but if it comes back we will try to follow it," Jessica said.

When the bat came back, it went straight for a monarch butterfly fairy that was resting on the branch of a bush. The children watched quietly, and then when the butterfly fairy got on the bat, the children quietly followed the bat to see where it would go. It went to the far end of the field and inside a hollow log.

The children hid behind a fallen tree and watched the bat as it went inside, and then it came back out and headed across the field. The children had to decide what to do next. They could go see if the other butterfly fairies and moth fairies were all inside and make sure they were okay, or they could go get Ambrosia and tell her what they had found.

Jessica argued that they should go and tell Ambrosia and see what she thought they should do. After all, if the bats had turned against the butterfly fairies and the moth fairies, then they may attack the children; and even though they were nectar bats, they may still bite.

There is no telling how many of them there are. Joey argued he thought it was the same bat they kept seeing over and over. But he had to agree he was not sure. Katie just did not know what to do. She was so worried that the bat had harmed the poor fairies. Katie never did like bats of any kind, so it was not a surprise to her that the bats were responsible for the missing fairies. After a lot of discussion on what to do, the children decided to go tell Ambrosia, and then they would follow her advice.

When they arrived back to Ambrosia, she was very upset. She had not seen the children when they had left and was afraid they had been captured as well. Jessica told her she was sorry but they did not have time to inform her of what they were doing.

"We saw who is taking the fairies, and we also saw where they have been taken to. We followed a nectar bat as it coaxed a fairy onto its back and then took her away," Jessica explained.

"That is impossible," stated Ambrosia. "The nectar bats have always been friends to the fairies for as long as I can remember. So I just can't see them turning on us. You must be mistaken."

"No, I am sorry, but we are not mistaken. We saw the bat come back over and over taking the fairies, then we followed the bat to see where it would go. It placed the fairies in a hollow tree, and the fairies did not come back out. Then the bat would go back and take another," Katie explained.

"Well," Ambrosia said. "We will wait until daylight when the bats go to sleep, and then we can go to this hollow log and see what is going on. Perhaps the fairies are okay and can tell us why the bats have done what they have. I still do not understand why the bats would turn on us this way. They have always treated us so good and have been very helpful. This really makes me sad to think they would do this to us. You children, get some rest. It is nearly 3 a.m. I will wake you all up at 6 a.m. We will try to find out then what is going on."

The children all agreed and headed for their tents.

"It may rain. Let's put our sleeping bags into the tents so we don't get wet." They all agreed, and surprisingly they were all asleep within minutes of lying down.

Around 6 a.m. Ambrosia came and woke the children. "It is time. I don't see any bats around." The children were very tired but they were also anxious to find out why the nectar bats were taking the moth and butterfly fairies. The children rolled up their sleeping bags and took down the tents. Then they were ready to go. When the children got to the hollow log in the dead tree they stopped. It was very scary. They did not know what to expect. What if the bat had hurt or even killed the fairies. What if the bat had seen the children and moved all the fairies. Ambrosia told the children to surround the log, and then she had Joey lift the log up. When he did, it came off the tree, and they could see all the fairies. There were hundreds of them. They were very surprised to see Ambrosia. The bat was still nowhere around. Ambrosia was even more surprised to see all the fairies.

"What is going on?" she asked. The fairies began to explain what had happened.

A very large monarch butterfly flew up to Ambrosia and began the story. A nectar bat had brought them to the stump one at a time. It had told them if they tried to escape he would capture their whole family, and so they had not tried to escape.

"It seemed the bat wanted one fairy from each of the families. He was trying to break some sort of spell that had been placed on the monarch butterflies many hundreds of years before. The bat believed he needed many of the butterfly fairies to break the spell."

"What about the moth fairies, why has he captured them as well?" the children asked.

"Because he feels they may hold some secrets of what he is looking for."

"Well, come on, we have to get you all out of here while he is gone," Joey said.

"No," they all shouted, "we can't. Or he will come after us again and take our families."

Jessica asked, "When does he usually come to take the fairies?"

The monarch stated, "Usually around 6 p.m., just before dark."

"Okay, then we will be here at 6 p.m. and talk to the bat. We will find out why he is doing this, what spell he expects to break. Maybe we can help him and then free the fairies," Jessica stated.

The other children agreed, and they decided to go home, get some rest, and meet at the field at 5:30 p.m. to plan their rescue.

Chapter 5

Kings and Monarchs

The children arrived at the wildflower field at exactly 5:30 p.m., ready to try to rescue the fairies. They were frightened; they did not know what was in store for them once they got to the dead tree and the hollow log. It was very quiet as the children walked through the field. No one said a word. Each child was thinking about what they thought was going to happen, and they were each trying to figure out what the bat was going to say. Jessica broke the silence. She began to tell the others what she thought was the reason for what the bat had done.

"The bat was bored. I think he collected all the fairies to enjoy and keep for himself. He has them all captive and plans to keep it that way."

"No, I think that he has become tired of carrying the fairies around all the time and has decided it was time for them to carry him around. So he is collecting enough of them that they could carry his weight. It is just his way of getting back at them for making him work the way he has."

The girls looked at Joey. "Well what do you think?" the girls asked together. Joey just stood there, looking very sad and worried.

"I don't know what to think, but I just hope we get there before something bad happens." And with that, they all continued walking without saying another word.

When they arrived at the dead tree, the bat was already there. It was just coming out of the opening. Joey ran over to it, and stopped it from leaving.

Joey shouted, "Stop where you are! What have you done with the fairies? We are on to you; we saw you stealing them and demand you to release them now and explain yourself." Katie and Jessica just stared at him. They could not believe their ears. Joey had never been so demanding before. They could tell he was very upset and worried.

Ambrosia flew up to the bat and asked, "How could you do this? We thought you were our friend. Why would you betray us this way?" The nectar bat looked very sad. He told the children and Ambrosia to have a seat. It was a long story.

"My name is Charlie," the nectar bat began. "I have been living in this wildflower field for the past five months. I have been searching for the monarch butterflies because they are truly kings. Have you never wondered where the name *monarch* came from? See, they were real kings and queens at one time. An evil being came along and changed them into butterflies, but because they were really human, they became fairies. Half butterfly, half human."

"Where did you hear such a story?" Ambrosia asked.

Charlie stated, "My family has passed the story down from generation to generation since I can remember."

"So you feel that the monarch butterflies are actually kings and queens, and you are here capturing them in the hope of turning them back to kings and queens?"

"Yes, that is it. I found a man whom I befriended, and he told me that he can change them back into their true selves."

"How did you, a bat, meet and start talking to a man?" Joey asked.

"I was pollinating the moonflowers, and the man caught me. I panicked and tried to get away, but he held me strong. I even tried to bite him. Finally, I stopped and looked at him, trying to figure out why he had a hold of me. He looked at me so calmly and asked me what my name was. I told him, and then he said he wanted to be my friend. He asked me a lot of questions about where I come from and about my family. He found my story about the kings and queens being changed into monarchs very interesting. He told me could change them back into there true selves if I found them and caught them all. I agreed to do that."

"Can you take us to see the man? It might help us if we can talk to the man. We really want to find out what his plan was and why he wanted you to capture the fairies."

Charlie agreed to take Katie, Jessica, Joey, and Ambrosia to see the man.

"Where does he live?" Jessica asked the bat.

"I don't know, but he is always at the park at the end of the block. He feeds the pigeons and the ducks."

The children agreed to go immediately to the park and see the man. Jessica was really scared. What was the man up to? Why did he want the fairies?

"That is him," Charlie said. The children walked bravely up to the man and said hello. The man stopped feeding the pigeons and said hello to the children. Then he saw the bat, and a smile appeared on his face.

"Hello, Charlie," the man said. "What brings you here? I thought you would be out playing with the butterflies."

"These are my new friends, and they want to know how you plan to change the butterflies back into kings and queens. Would you please explain it to them?"

The man just looked at Charlie. Then he looked a little sad. Joey looked at the man and said, "You don't know anything about changing them back, do you?"

"No," the man said. "I don't know anything about it. I talked to the bat, and he seemed excited about changing the butterflies into kings and queens. I knew that if he thought I could change them he would keep coming back to see me. I did not really think he would go out and capture all the butterflies." "Did you hurt them?" the man asked.

"No," said Charlie. "But why would you say that you could help if you did not know anything about it and could not help at all?"

"I just wanted a friend. You were the first bat I found that could talk to me. And it was so exciting. I'm sorry. They are just butterflies though, and there are plenty of them. Please forgive me, bat, I really just wanted to be your friend."

Katie looked at Charlie; he looked so sad. "Charlie," Katie said, "don't be so upset. Maybe many, many years ago the monarch butterflies really were kings and queens, but that was so long ago, and now they are really butterflies. They would not know where to go or how to live if they were changed. I think just being a beautiful butterfly is all they know how to do, and they do it so well. I also think it is time to go set them free. If you tell them why you captured them, I think they will forgive you and may not even be mad. Let's go try it and see. Okay?"

"Okay," Charlie agreed.

The children, Ambrosia, and Charlie headed back to the field. Charlie accepted the apology and promised he would come back to visit the man often.

When the children and the bat and the moth all got back to the wildflower field, they went straight to the dead tree with the hollow log. Charlie, the bat, called into the log for the butterflies to come out. Slowly, they began to come out of the log. They looked nervous. They were also very hungry; they had not had anything to eat or drink in days.

Charlie saw how badly they looked, and he felt so bad. "I am so sorry," he said. "I don't know how I can ever make this right." He went and got them some water and carried them one at a time to the flowers. Soon the butterfly fairies and moth fairies began to feel a little better. Charlie asked them to all sit down so he could tell them what was going on.

"I don't know where to begin," started Charlie. "I have heard stories since I was a child about how the kings and queens of the olden days all being changed into monarch butterflies. *Monarch*, you see, means 'king'."

The butterflies explained that they had always been told that when a group of people came over to the United States and they saw the butterflies for the first time they thought they were so beautiful so they named them monarch or some even called them King Billy. We always thought it was such a pretty story. But we never heard about the story you told. We have to say we agree that you did do this to try to help, but we like our lives the way we are. We really do appreciate that you wanted to help. We do not hate you. Nobody got hurt, and we can go home to our families now."

The children were relieved that the mystery was over and that all the butterfly and moth fairies were safe and sound where they belonged. The children all agreed it was time for them to be going home.

Chapter 6

The Secret of the Lunar Moth

The next day, when Jessica woke up it was nearly 10 a.m. She was tired from all the excitement of the last few days. She called Katie to find out what she was doing. Katie's mother told Jessica that Katie was still in bed asleep. Katie never slept so late, but Jessica knew they had been through a lot in the past few days and felt it was probably a good thing they caught up on sleep. She asked Katie's mother to have Katie call her when she woke up.

Jessica did not do much all morning, watched a little bit of cartoons, and played with her guinea pig. Finally, around eleven thirty, Katie called and asked Jessica to come over. Joey was already there when Jessica arrived.

"What's up?" Jessica asked.

"We are trying to decide what to do this evening."

"What do you mean?" Jessica asked. "We are going to the field, aren't we?"

"Yes," Katie said. "But what time do we go, and how late can we stay? We have to come up with a reason to go. My mom keeps asking why we go so much and what we do there and stuff like that."

"Well, I would like to go around 4:30 p.m. I'd like to see the moonflowers open. I just can't get enough of that. Ambrosia promised to tell us a secret about her. So it should be a very interesting evening."

The others agreed. and they planned to meet at the field at four thirty. They would tell their parents the truth. They were going to the wildflower field to watch the moths and butterflies.

It was a very hot afternoon, and none of the children wanted to go outside to play or do anything. Joey suggested they just stay inside and play video games and relax. Katie's mom brought in some cookies and Kool-Aid. Before they realized what time it was, it was nearly 4 p.m. Jessica and Joey said they needed to go home and get ready to go to the field. They said their goodbyes and left. They all asked if it was okay to go to the field to play for the evening. The children explained they were going to pick wildflowers to put in their houses. That was the best excuse; none of their parents questioned further than that.

The children met at the field as they agreed. They set out a blanket in front of the wildflowers at four thirty, as they had planned. The field was busy with the monarch butterfly fairies flying from flower to flower. Every now and then, one would fly over to one of the children and talk to them.

The fairies loved to laugh and could be heard laughing and playing around the fields. The children loved to watch them play and fly from flower to flower. Around five thirty, the moonflowers began to open at once. They made a sudden popping sound as they all opened at the same time. The children sat there and waited to see if Ambrosia would show up. She always did come to see them, but now the children were just unsure of whether she was coming.

Finally, she did show up. The children were so happy. They all began to talk to her all at the same time.

"Well," began Ambrosia, "I have a story to tell you tonight. This is going to surprise you. As you know, I am a lunar moth. My species only live about two weeks. No one has ever documented a moth of my species living for over a month span; however, I am thirteen years old. When I first found this field, I was only about a week old. I met a lunar moth who explained to me she had lived for thirty years. She told me that her job was to watch over the field and protect the fairies that came to the field to live. The moth also told me that she had lived way beyond any moth ever, and that now it was my turn. She explained to me that she wanted me to take over and protect all the inhabitants of the field. I was honored to be offered such an important job. The moth's name was

Shallena; she was larger and smarter than most of the lunar moths in the field. She explained that the lunars got their name because they could fly at night. Lunar moths, like the famous sphinx moths, could keep their thoughts and intentions secret, which was very important in taking care of such a large population and all the problems that they may have. Shallena explained to me that there had been so many problems that had occurred, but she had held strong and helped the others to get through them all.

"The most exciting story Shallena told me was about a dream that one day, three young humans would come to the field. When these humans showed up at the field, they would help with a crisis that was going on. She also explained to me that I must trust these humans and allow them to know all our secrets, and they would help us. When you caught me, I was terrified. All I could think about was saving my life. I did not think about you being the children I had been told about. When Jessica released me, then I knew you must be the ones fulfilling a dream long ago told. I was so excited. I am very glad we became friends. Just as was foretold, you did help when we needed it most. By releasing the monarch butterfly fairies and the moth fairies, you did it. I am so pleased that it was during my lifetime that you came. I do hope that we will be able to be friends for a very long time."

The children all agreed at once that they would all be friends for a very long time.

With that, Katie reminded the others that it was time to go home. They said their good-byes and thanked the lunar moth fairy for telling them the wonderful story. Then the children left to go home.

Chapter 7

Fairy Dust

The next morning, Jessica woke up at 7:30 a.m. She wondered what they would do for the day. Their summer had been so exciting so far; she could not imagine how they would get through the rest of the summer now that the excitement was over. Oh sure they would go back to the wildflower field and see all the fairies, but now it was a natural everyday thing.

Not exciting as it was at the beginning. Nothing else will probably happen to change that.

Jessica had been lying in her bed for nearly thirty minutes thinking about what she and the other children could possibly do for fun when Katie and Joey both showed up. Apparently, they had been thinking the same thing.

They all agreed they would go to the field and have a picnic supper that evening. They also agree to meet at four thirty like they used to so they could watch the moonflowers as they opened. They all still agreed that watching the moonflowers open was a very exciting thing to see and could not see it enough. Jessica's mother cooked chocolate chip pancakes for the children. They were so good, everyone asked for seconds.

After breakfast, Katie's mother called and asked if the kids would like to go to the county swimming pool. They were all very excited at the idea of going to the pool. It was showing the possibility of being a very hot day. The thermometer outside read a blistering 90 degrees and it was only 9 a.m. Katie said she believed the temperature would probably be over 100 degrees by lunchtime.

Swimming was the only thing they could do other than sit in an air-conditioned house. Katie and Joey left to go get their swimming suits and towels ready. Jessica agreed to meet them in thirty minutes at Katie's house. By 9:30 a.m., all the children were ready and loaded into Katie's mother's minivan.

They reached the pool at 10 a.m. It was already getting crowded. An hour later, the pool was filled to capacity, and the front desk was sending people away.

Katie, Joey, and Jessica played Marco Polo for hours along with other children from the neighborhood.

Katie's mother called the children out of the pool at noon for lunch. She had brought tuna sandwiches and Capri Suns. The children were all hungry. They sat at a table with an umbrella and enjoyed their lunch and drinks. After lunch, Katie's mother stated they had to wait thirty minutes before they could go back into the pool. They had waited the amount of time necessary, and then the children all went back into the pool. At two thirty, Katie's mom said it was time to go.

The children decided to go to their own homes and relax awhile, change clothes, and meet back at the wildflower field at four thirty. They also decided they would each bring their own meal and have a picnic at the field for supper.

Jessica arrived at the wildflower field first. Ambrosia, the lunar moth, was waiting for her. She told Jessica that the monarch butterfly fairies had a surprise for the children.

"Have you ever heard of fairy dust?" she asked.

"Yes, but it is only make-believe, isn't it?" Jessica asked.

"Oh no, it most definitely is not only make-believe; you are in for a real treat tonight."

Jessica could hardly wait for Katie and Joey to show up. When they did, she started explaining excitedly about the fairy dust and that the butterfly fairies had some for the children.

"What will it do?" Joey asked.

"I don't know," Jessica said, but it has to be wonderful.

With that, the monarch butterfly fairy showed up with the fairy dust.

"With this fairy dust you will be able to fly," the monarch butterfly said.

"Oh," said Joey, "that is cool, but we already got to fly with the dew from the moonflowers. I thought we would be able to do something different."

"Well," said the fairy, "I did not finish; I said that you would be able to fly, but you will also turn into fairies when I sprinkle the fairy dust on your head."

"Wow," all the children said in unison. "That is special. It sounds like a lot of fun. How long would we be fairies? We would be able to turn back into our human shape again, wouldn't we? I mean fairies are wonderful, but we like being kids too."

"Yes," said the fairy, "you will become human again." "The fairy dust only last for one hour from the time you sprinkle it on your head," the fairy explained.

"When can we have a sprinkle of fairy dust put on our head?" Joey asked.

"Now," said the fairy, "if you are ready."

The children all agreed they were ready. And the fairy began to sprinkle a pretty glittery dust on each of their heads.

One by one, the children became fairies. They laughed at each other at how they looked. Then they all began to fly up and around the flowers. Jessica was so excited she even went to the flower and drank it, as she had seen the moth and butterfly fairies do. This was so incredible she had never believed she could be flying and actually even be a fairy. It was so wonderful; she felt so free, as if she could go anywhere or do anything. The children one by one flew up and around the flowers and the trees. It was like nothing they had ever imagined. They dipped in between the flowers and flew over the hedges. None of the children wanted this wonderful experience to ever end.

Then some of the monarch butterfly fairies came over and told the children fairies to follow them. They took the children to the end of the wildflower field and showed them a beautiful creek that flowed right around the edges.

The children were surprised; they did not know that the creek was there. The butterfly fairies showed the children how to fly down close to the water and actually get their wings wet as they dipped in and out near the water. The water was cool; it felt great to get wet in the hot afternoon sun. It was surprising how cool it actually felt just to fly around; the movement of the wings seem to help keep the fairies cool.

The children continued to fly around the wildflowers and in and out of the creek. They flew for hours. It was so much fun they forgot to watch the time. Suddenly, Jessica realized that it must be very late; she flew over to one of the monarch butterfly fairies and asked how they could become human again.

"Why?" asked the butterfly fairy. "Are you tired of being a fairy?"

"No, no," Jessica stated. "It is just that it is getting very late, and we are probably in trouble already; we have to get home. Our parents may be out looking for us already. You had told us the dust only worked for one hour, but it must have been many hours already."

"One of the best parts about being a fairy, which includes the fairy dust, is that in our world time moves very slowly. That is why even though our lifespan is only weeks, we have a full life. Time moves at a speed of about 1/10th of the time of yours. In your time, it has only been minutes. Although in our time, it has seemed like three or four hours. So you see, there is no hurry. You can fly for as long as you like. You will be tired long before you will be late getting home."

"That is great," said Jessica, and with that she continued to fly around.

It was very difficult finding Katie and Joey. They were so little, and the world suddenly seemed like such a large place. Jessica was starting to look very sad, and a butterfly fairy saw her and came over right away and asked what is wrong.

"You look so sad," said the fairy. "What is wrong? Is there anything I can do to help?"

"No," said Jessica. "I just want to find my friends, but the world is so big and they are so small I don't know where to even start looking."

"Oh well, that is easy," said the fairy. "You just make a call like this." And with that the fairy made a loud shrill sound. In just seconds, Katie and Joey both flew to Jessica.

"Wow, that was so fast," Jessica said. "I can't believe how well that works."

"Don't you remember how the lunar moth fairy called out to the butterfly and moth fairies the day she let us meet them?" Katie asked.

"Yes, I do, but I didn't know that it would work for us as well."

"So why did you call for us?" Katie asked.

"I was just thinking about you; we had been flying around for so long I was just starting to really worry because I had not seen you for so long. And I didn't know how I'd ever find you both now that we are so small."

Joey started to explain to the girls that time moves much slower in fairy time than human time. But the girls stopped him and explained that they both had already found out that information. The children all decided to fly around the flowers for a little longer, and then they would head for home. The children would be changed back into their human forms first, of course.

Chapter 8

Hiding Places

The next morning Jessica slept in until nearly 10 a.m. She was very tired after all the exiting things she had done the day before. Actually, she was tired from the wonderful summer vacation. The children had been so busy and had such a wild summer that she felt nothing could ever compare to the experiences she had been through. It had definitely been a wonderful summer. Jessica knew there was only a few more days of summer left and she would have to say good-bye to Katie and Joey and the fairies. She wondered if the fairies would be in the field next year. Of course, it would be all new fairies by then, and they would not even know who she was.

Jessica decided to call and see what Katie and Joey were doing. Katie was still asleep, but Joey was out working in his workshop. *He must be working on the fairy-house surprise for the fairies*, thought Jessica. *I am going over there and see if I can help*. Jessica went over to Joey's house, and sure enough, he was working on the surprise.

"Can I help?" Jessica asked.

"Sure, just hand me those boards. These are going to be hiding homes for the fairies. I think if I make about twelve that should be enough to hide the butterfly fairies during the night and the moonflower moth fairies during the day," Joey explained.

"How many of them did you make so far?" Jessica asked.

"I have made eight of them so far, but I have to finish them before the end of the week. We are going home early this year. My dad has to be back at work sooner than usual, and it is causing us to have to leave nearly a week earlier than usual. So I would be thankful for any help you and Katie could give me," Joey stated.

"I was wondering if I should paint them too. I thought something nice like the flowers they all love would be great, but I'm thinking maybe camouflage would be better to help them hide easier. So predators and people would not spot them when they are sleeping. See I also have made the door hole very small so the birds will not be able to get in. What do you think?" Joey asked.

"I think this is the best idea you ever had. I really like the design too. Let's call Katie and get her over her and get these hiding places made for our friends, the fairies," Jessica stated. Joey agreed. Jessica called Katie from Joey's house and explained about Joey having to go home early, that he had been making the hiding places, but they were incomplete. He was asking for their help to finish the product, and then they would present them to the fairies together. Katie agreed and said she would be right over to help.

A few minutes later, Katie arrived at Joey's house ready to help with the houses. Together they all nailed the roofs to walls and floors. They decided to paint the houses camouflage and covered them with a special spray that would help them to retain the paint job longer and hold up in all kinds of weather; now each summer when the new fairies arrived, they would be able to have a safe place to sleep. It took all day to finish the houses that were left and to paint the ones that Joey had already built.

The children could hardly wait to give them to the fairies. They just knew that the fairies were going to love the houses. It was late when they finished the houses. The children all agreed they would take them to the fairies the very next day. Katie and Jessica said good night and left to go home.

Jessica was so excited about giving the houses to the fairies that she found it very hard to sleep. Each time she fell asleep, she would dream about the fairies and the hiding places. She dreamed of flying as a girl and flying as a fairy. She would dream of diving up and around flowers and into the stream. When she woke up between dreams, she found it hard to fall back asleep; she could not stop thinking about the most wonderful and enchanting summer she ever had. Finally, it was morning, and Katie was calling Jessica to go to the field and give the fairies the houses. The girls called Joey, and they agreed to meet at his house and put the houses in a wagon and take them to the field.

After loading all the houses into an old wagon, the children headed for the wildflower field. They were very excited they could hardly wait to see the reaction when they gave the fairies the houses. The fairies were delighted when the children presented them with the houses.

"They are beautiful," the fairies shouted.

"I can't believe you did this for us."

The children set forth at once to hang the houses where the fairies wanted them. The houses were placed all around the wildflower field. The sphinx and lunar moths awoke to see the wonderful houses and were very eager to go into them and sleep for the day. The butterfly fairies all agreed they would sleep in them that night. They thanked the children for the most wonderful gift they had ever received. The children were satisfied. They knew they had done one last thing for the fairies before summer was over. Soon they would be going home and back to school. They promised Ambrosia (the lunar moth) they would come back that evening to see her. She had something she wanted to talk to them about.

Chapter 9

Friendships Forever

The children had agreed to meet at the wildflower field at 4:30 p.m., just as they had at the beginning, and watch the moonflowers as they opened. The children were a bit sad; they knew that when they left, the moth fairies and butterfly fairies would die at the end of the summer, and they would be gone forever. The children had been having so much fun they hated for it to come to such an end.

At four thirty, the children arrived at the field. They set their blanket up like they had so many times before. Soon the moonflowers did their nightly show of opening all at once, and then *pop*, they were all opened. Tonight the children found even this hard to enjoy. After the flowers opened, Ambrosia showed up.

"Why all the sad faces?" she asked.

Katie explained to Ambrosia what was bothering them.

"Oh," Ambrosia said. "I guess you still don't understand, do you?"

The children all looked at the lunar moth, confused.

"Understand what?" the children all asked the moth fairy at the same time.

"Well, sit down please, and I will explain it to you from the beginning.

"There is a legend that has been passed down from summer to summer through each life line of butterfly and moth fairies. The legend says that there are three human children who will come one day and help the fairies in many ways. When you captured me and then turned me loose the way you did, I knew right then that you were the chosen ones. And I was right, look at all the things you have done this summer for us."

Jessica was unsure about her being a chosen one, so she asked Ambrosia, "If I am a chosen one, then why didn't I see you last year? My family came here, and I came to this field at that time. Joey and Katie and I met in this field last year."

"Well, I guess you were not old enough at that time. I remember watching you three play over at the edge of the field many times last year. I wondered if you were the chosen ones, but I could not do anything I had to wait and see."

The children were so surprised by what Ambrosia was telling them. They never considered the idea that they were part of a legend. Ambrosia had already told them the legend once, but they still felt it was only pretend or if true it could not be about them.

Katie looked at Ambrosia with tears in her eyes and said, "So what is it all for? I mean when we leave for the summer the moth and butterfly fairies will all die and none will know us next year when we come back."

"I will still be here, child. I will never forget you and the things you have done and who you are will be implanted into the fairies memories; like DNA, it will be passed on summer after summer. Every year that you come, you will have adventures. The moth and butterfly fairies will be even more excited waiting for you to arrive, then you will."

The children were so happy they could hardly believe that they would not be forgotten and that their adventures would continue summer after summer. Suddenly, the children were all smiling and laughing and playing.

Jessica turned to Ambrosia and asked, "How long has this legend been around? I mean, did it start when you were born or did someone tell you about?"

Ambrosia looked at Jessica. "You are always so full of questions" She smiled at Jessica and said, "The legend has been passed down for over a hundred years. Long before you were even born, long before your parents were born. So you see, you are a part of something so much bigger."

Jessica sat there thinking. It is so hard to imagine that a legend had been told about her and her friends long before they were even born. But Jessica knew one thing. She sure was glad that the legend was true and that it was about her and her friends.

Ambrosia told the children that the fairies wanted to have an end-of-summer party for the children. That it was going to be the next evening at 5 p.m. The fairies and the children knew it would be their last time together for the summer, but they were all looking forward to it as well. The children said good night and went home for supper. The rest of the evening was spent doing quieter activities. Katie was watching TV, Joey was playing X-Box, and Jessica, of course, was reading books.

The next day, the children got together after breakfast and went swimming at Katie's. It was another hot day. Swimming felt so wonderful; her pool was small, but it felt great. Of course, the children all agreed that swimming was not as much fun as flying, but it was wonderful and cool. The children were all excellent swimmers.

Soon it was lunchtime, and they headed home for lunch. The children spent a quiet afternoon at their own homes. They could not stop thinking about the wonderful fairies.

At five o'clock the children all arrived at the field as they had promised. And to their surprise, there were more fairies than they had ever seen. And even the birds came to edge of the fields and sang. The nectar bats were swooshing all around. The sounds the different insects, birds, and bats made sounded like music. The children realized it was really a party. And this party was in their honor. The children laughed and ran and played with the fairies for as long as they could, but as always, it became dark, and they had to say their farewells. The fairies all said good-bye and wished the children a wonderful year. The children all promised they would definitely try.

Jessica looked at Ambrosia and told her how much she was going to miss her and all the rest of the moth and butterfly fairies.

"Well, we will definitely miss you too, but you know that you can also talk to the fireflies, right?" Ambrosia asked.

Jessica looked at her, "What do you mean? How would we talk to fireflies?"

"You do have fireflies around your home, don't you?" Ambrosia asked.

"Yes we do," the children all said at once. "But we have never talked to them."

"I have caught many fireflies but they do not look like fairies and none of them have ever tried to talk to me," Joey stated.

"Have you ever tried to talk to them?" Ambrosia asked.

"Well no," admitted Joey. "But then again, I never really thought about it either."

"Well, when you get home, go out one evening and try talking to them. You may be surprised," Ambrosia told the children.

The children said their good-byes for the summer. They promised Ambrosia they would look for her when they came back next summer. They all admitted that they could hardly wait to see the fairies again.

When the children arrived back at their summer homes, they had to pack and get ready to leave. The children all said there good-byes and promised to call each other at least once a week. They also promised to keep each other informed of how things were going with the fireflies. If we can talk to butterflies, moths, and fireflies, there is no telling what other wonderful creatures we can talk too.

When Jessica arrived at her house, the first thing she did was ask her mother to take her to the library to check out a book on fireflies. She wanted to learn all she could about the fireflies before she tried to talk to them. She had a feeling she might be in for another wonderful adventure.